Easy Anti-Inflammatory Cookbook for Beginners

Cheap and Fast Delicacies for your Everyday Dishes

Thomas Jollif

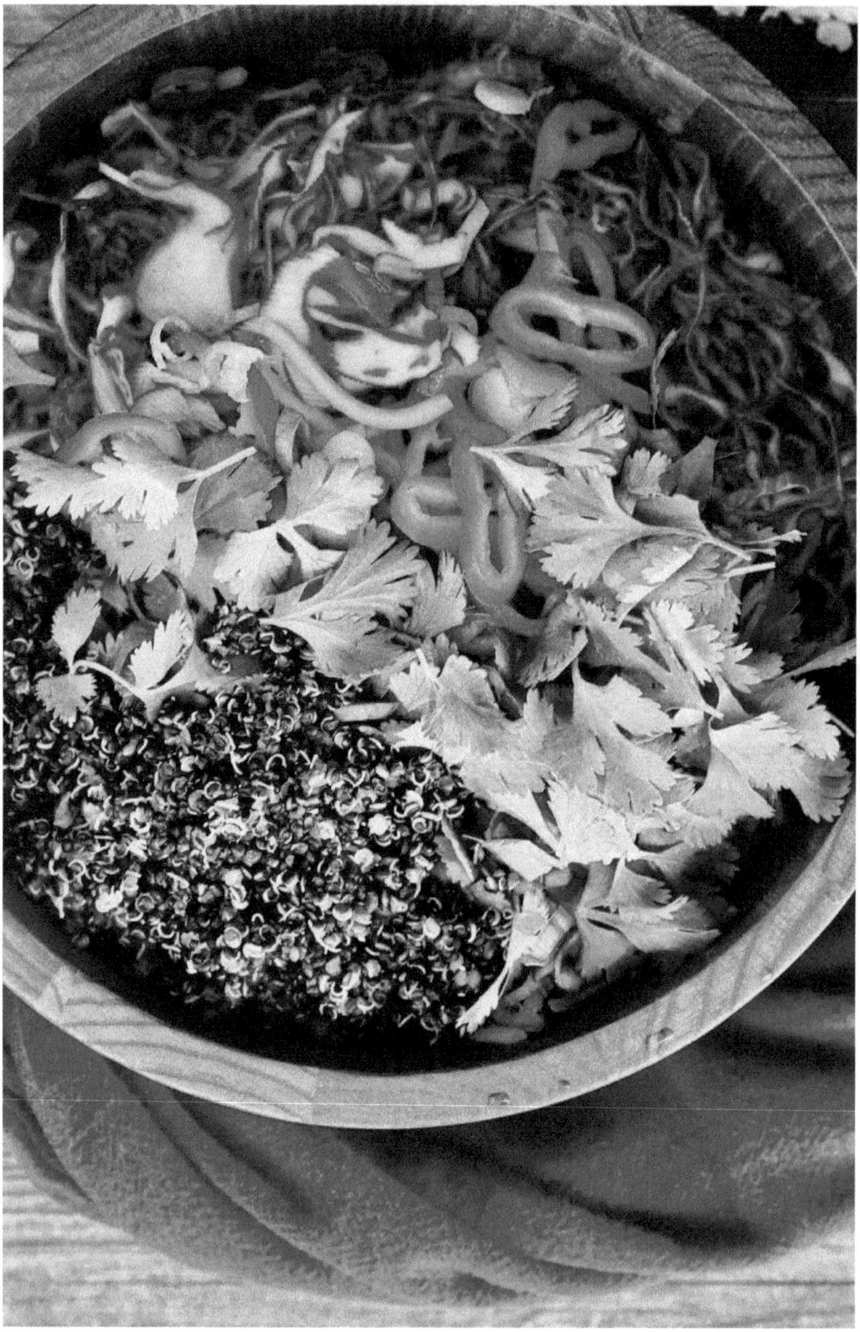

by reading this document, the reader agrees that under no circumstances is the author responsible for any losses, direct or indirect, which are incurred as a result of the use of information contained within this document, including, but not limited to, — errors, omissions, or inaccuracies.

Table of Contents

BREAKFASTS

Tuna & Sweet Potato Croquettes

Time To Prepare: fifteen minutes

Time to Cook: twelve minutes

Yield: Servings 8

Ingredients:

- ¼ cup almond flour
- ¼ cup tapioca flour
- ¼ teaspoon garam masala
- ¼ teaspoon ground turmeric
- ¼ teaspoon red chili powder
- ½ big onion, chopped
- ½ teaspoon ground coriander
- 1 (1-inch piece fresh ginger, minced
- 1 cup sweet potato, peeled and mashed
- 1 egg
- 1 Serrano pepper, seeded and minced
- 1 tablespoon coconut oil
- 2 (5 oz.) cans tuna
- 3 garlic cloves, minced
- Freshly ground black pepper, to taste

- Olive oil, as required
- Salt, to taste

Directions:

1. In a frying pan, warm the coconut oil on moderate heat.
2. Put onion, ginger, garlic, and Serrano pepper and sauté for roughly 5-6 minutes.
3. Mix in spices and sauté roughly one minute more.
4. Move the onion mixture in a container.
5. Put in tuna and sweet potato and mix till well blended.
6. Make equal sized oblong shaped patties in the mixture.
7. Position the croquettes inside a baking sheet in a very single layer and place in your fridge for overnight.
8. In a shallow dish, beat the egg.
9. In another shallow dish, combine both flours.
10. In a big frying pan, heat the enough oil.
11. Put in croquettes in batches and shallow fry for about two to three minutes per side.

Nutritional Info: Calories: 404 ‖ Fat: 9g ‖ Carbohydrates: 20g ‖ Fiber: 4g ‖ Protein: 30g

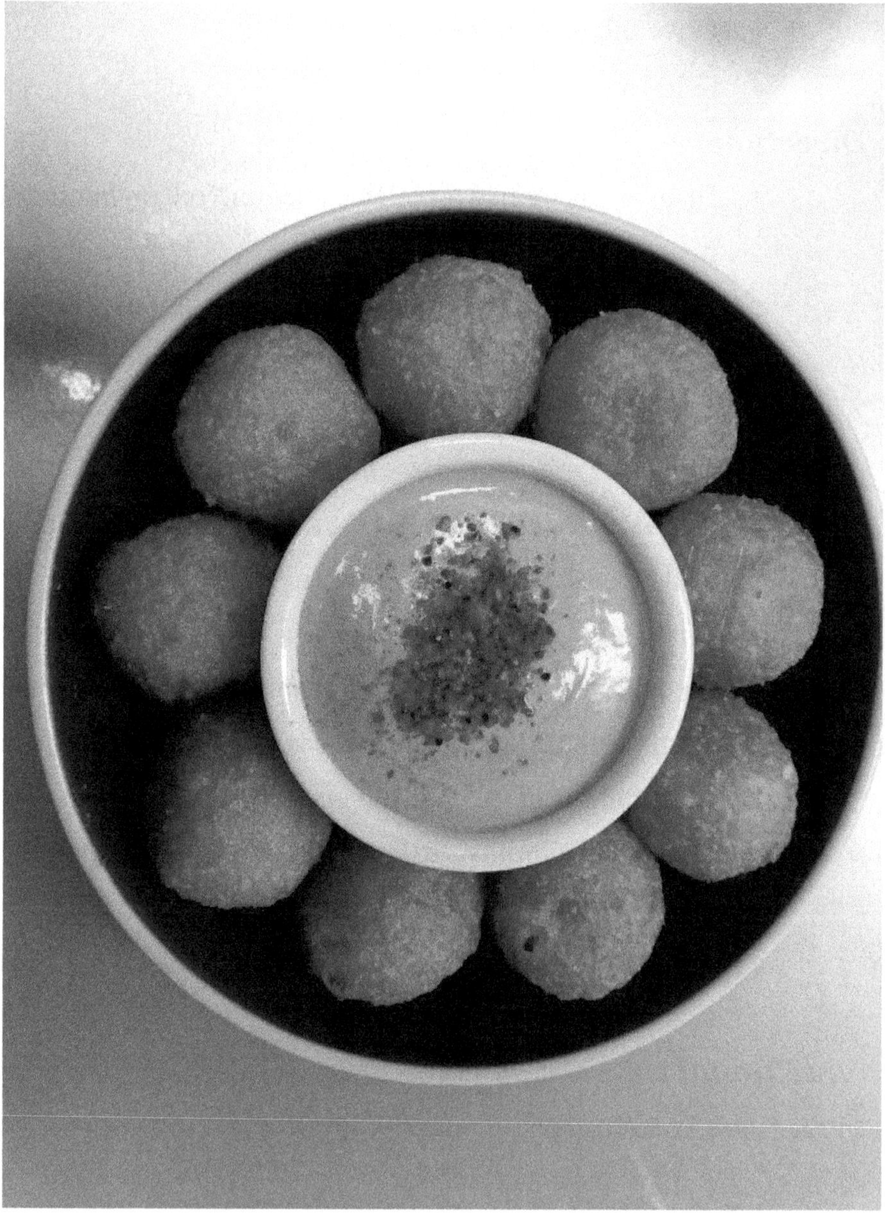

Turkey Burgers

Time To Prepare: fifteen minutes

Time to Cook: 8 minutes

Yield: Servings 5

Ingredients:

- 1 ripe pear, peeled, cored and chopped roughly
- 1 teaspoon fresh ginger, grated finely
- 1 teaspoon fresh rosemary, minced
- 1 teaspoon fresh sage, minced
- 1-2 tablespoons coconut oil
- 1-pound lean ground turkey
- 2 minced garlic cloves
- Freshly ground black pepper, to taste
- Salt, to taste

Directions:

1. In a blender, put in pear and pulse till smooth.
2. Move the pear mixture in a big container with rest of the ingredients except for oil and mix till well blended.
3. Make small equal sized 10 pattics from the mixture.
4. In a heavy-bottomed frying pan, heat oil on moderate heat.
5. Put in the patties and cook for about five minutes.
6. Flip the inside and cook for roughly 2-3 minutes.

Nutritional Info: Calories: 477 ‖ Fat: 15g ‖ Carbohydrates: 26g ‖ Fiber: 11g ‖ Protein: 35g

Vegan-Friendly Banana Bread

Time To Prepare: fifteen minutes

Time to Cook: forty minutes

Yield: Servings 4-6

Ingredients:

- 2 ripe bananas, mashed
- 3 tbsp. chia seeds
- 6 tbsp. water
- ½ cup tender vegan butter
- ½ cup maple syrup
- 2 cups flour
- 2 tsp. baking powder
- 1 tsp. cinnamon powder
- 1 tsp. allspice
- ½ tsp. salt
- 1/3 cup brewed coffee

Directions:

1. Set oven at 350F.
2. Bring the chia seeds in a small container then soak it with 6 tbsp. of water. Stir thoroughly and save for later.

3. In a mixing container, mix using a hand mixer the vegan butter and maple syrup until it turns fluffy. Put in the chia seeds together with the mashed bananas.
4. Mix thoroughly and then put in the coffee.
5. In the meantime, sift all the dry ingredients (flour, baking powder, cinnamon powder, all spice, and salt) and then progressively put in into the container with the wet ingredients.
6. Mix the ingredients well and then pour over a baking pan coated with parchment paper.
7. Put in your oven to bake for minimum 30-40 minutes, or until the toothpick comes out clean after inserting in the bread.
8. Let the bread cool before you serve.

Nutritional Info: Calories: 371 kcal ‖ Protein: 5.59 g ‖ Fat: 16.81 g ‖ Carbohydrates: 49.98 g

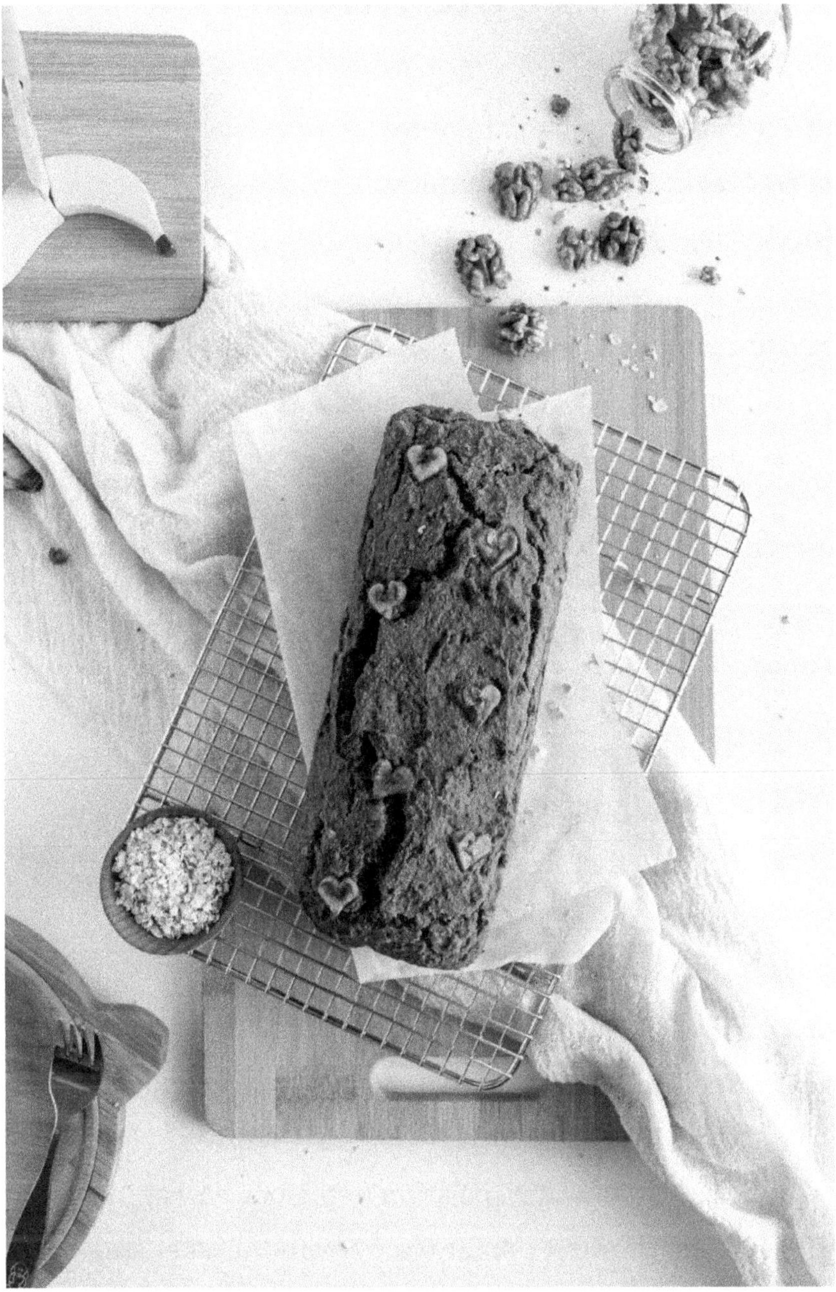

Veggie Balls

Time To Prepare: fifteen minutes

Time to Cook: twenty-five minutes

Yield: Servings 5-6

Ingredients:

- ¼ tsp. ground turmeric
- ½ teaspoon granulated garlic
- 1 cup fresh kale leaves, trimmed and chopped
- 1 medium shallot, chopped finely
- 1 tsp. ground cumin
- 2 medium sweet potatoes, cubed into ½-inch size
- 2 tablespoons coconut milk
- Freshly ground black pepper, to taste
- Ground flax seeds, as required
- Salt, to taste

Directions:

1. Set the oven to 400°F. Coat a baking sheet using parchment paper.
2. In a pan of water, position a steamer basket.
3. Bring the sweet potato in a steamer basket and steam roughly 10-fifteen minutes.

4. In a sizable container, put the sweet potato.

5. Put in coconut milk and purée well.

6. Put in rest of the ingredients except for flax seeds and mix till well blended.

7. Make approximately 1½-2-inch balls from your mixture.

8. Position the balls onto the readied baking sheet inside a single layer.

9. Drizzle with flax seeds.

10. Bake for around 20-twenty-five minutes.

Nutritional Info: Calories: 464 ‖ Fat: 12g ‖ Carbohydrates: 20g ‖ Fiber: 8g ‖ Protein: 27g

Weekend Breakfast Salad

Time To Prepare: thirty minutes

Time to Cook: 0 minutes

Yield: Servings 4

Ingredients:

- ½ cup Cucumber, chopped
- ½ cup Dill, chopped
- 1 cup Almonds, chopped
- 1 cup Quinoa, cooked and cooled
- 1 Large Avocado, cut thin
- 1 Large Tomato, cut in wedges
- 1 Lemon
- 10 cups Arugula
- 2 tbsp. Olive oil
- 4 Eggs, hard-boiled

Directions:

1. Mix together the quinoa, cucumber, tomatoes, and arugula. Toss these ingredients lightly with olive oil, salt, and pepper. Split the salad into 4 plates and position the egg and avocado on top. Top each salad with almonds and herbs.

2. Sprinkle with juice from the lemon.

Nutritional Info: Calories 336 ‖ 7.7 grams Fat ‖ 12.3 grams Protein ‖ 54.6 grams carbs ‖ 5.5 grams sugar ‖ 5.2 grams fiber ‖

White and Green Quiche

Time To Prepare: ten minutes

Time to Cook: forty minutes

Yield: Servings 3

Ingredients:

- 1 ½ cups of coconut milk
- 1 ½ teaspoon of baking powder
- 1 small sized onion, finely chopped
- 3 cloves of garlic, minced
- 3 cups of fresh spinach, chopped
- 5 white mushrooms, cut
- fifteen big free-range eggs
- Ghee, as required to grease the dish
- Ground black pepper to taste
- Sea salt to taste

Directions:

1. Set the oven to 350°F.
2. Get a baking dish then grease it with the organic ghee.
3. Break all the eggs in a huge container then whisk well.
4. Mix in coconut milk. Beat well

5. While you are whisking the eggs, start putting in the rest of the ingredients in it.

6. When all the ingredients are completely mixed, pour all of it into the readied baking dish.

7. Bake for minimum forty minutes, up to the quiche is set in the center.

8. Enjoy!

Nutritional Info: Calories: 608 kcal ‖ Protein: 20.28 g ‖ Fat: 53.42 g ‖ Carbohydrates: 16.88 g

Whole Grain Blueberry Scones

Time To Prepare: ten minutes

Time to Cook: twenty-five minutes

Yield: Servings 8

Ingredients:

- ¼ cup maple syrup
- ½ teaspoon sea salt
- 1 cup blueberries
- 1 teaspoon vanilla extract
- 2 cups of whole-wheat flour
- 2 tablespoons of coconut milk
- 2½ teaspoons baking powder
- 6 tablespoons of olive oil

Directions:

1. Set the oven 400°F. Place parchment paper on your baking sheet.
2. Put in the syrup, flour, salt, and baking powder in a container. Mix well by whisking together.
3. Pour the olive oil into a container with the dry ingredients.
4. Work the oil into your flour mix.

5. Mix the vanilla extract and coconut milk into the dry ingredients container.

6. Fold in the blueberries gently. Your dough must be sticky and thick.

7. Put some flour on your hand then mold the dough into a circle.

8. Use a knife to make triangle slices.

9. Place them over the baking sheet. Maintain an 8-inch gap.

10. Bake for about twenty-five minutes. Set aside on the baking sheet for cooling when finished.

Nutritional Info: Calories 331 ‖ Carbohydrates: 27g ‖ Cholesterol: 0mg ‖ Total Fat: 23g ‖ Protein: 4g ‖ Fiber: 4g ‖ Sugar: 8g

Yogurt Cheese and Fruit

Time To Prepare: ten minutes

Time to Cook: 0 minutes

Yield: Servings 6

Ingredients:

- ¼ cup dried cranberries or raisins
- ¼ cup honey
- ½ cup orange juice
- ½ cup water
- 1 fresh Golden Delicious apple
- 1 fresh pear
- 1 teaspoon fresh lemon juice
- 3 cups plain nonfat yogurt

Directions:

1. Prepare the yogurt cheese the day before by lining a colander or strainer with cheesecloth. Scoop the yogurt into the cheesecloth, put the strainer over a pot or container to catch the whey, and place in your fridge for minimum 8 hours before you serve.
2. In a huge mixing container, combine the juices and water. Chop the apple then pear into wedges, put the

wedges in the juice mixture, allow it to sit for minimum five minutes. Strain off the liquid.

3. When the yogurt is firm, remove from fridge, slice, and place on plates. Position the fruit wedges around the yogurt. Sprinkle   with honey and drizzle with cranberries or raisins just before you serve.

Nutritional Info: Calories: 177 ‖ Fat: 1 g ‖ Protein: 6.5 g ‖ Sodium: 87 mg ‖ Fiber: 2 g ‖ Carbohydrates: 35 g

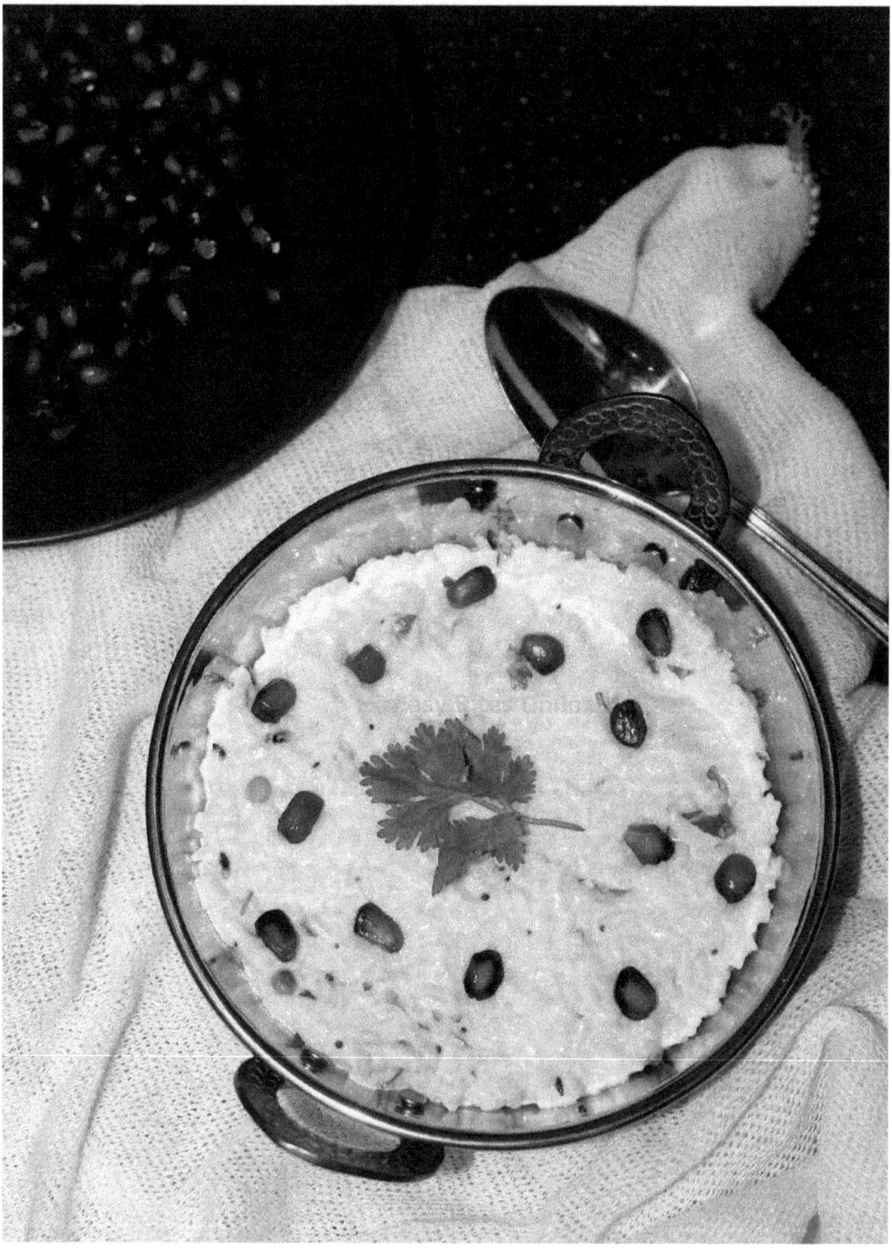

Yummy Steak Muffins

Time To Prepare: ten minutes

Time to Cook: twenty minutes

Yield: Servings 4

Ingredients:

- ¼ teaspoon of sea salt
- 1 cup of finely diced onion
- 1 cup red bell pepper, diced
- 2 Tablespoons of water
- 8 free-range eggs
- 8 ounce thin steak, cooked and finely chopped
- Dash of freshly ground black pepper

Directions:

1. Set the oven to 350°F
2. Take 8 muffin tins and line then using parchment paper liners.
3. Get a big container and crack all the eggs in it.
4. Beat well the eggs.
5. Blend in all the rest of the ingredients.
6. Ladle the batter into the position muffin tins. Fill three-fourth of each tin.

7. Place the muffin tins in the preheated oven for approximately twenty minutes, until the muffins are baked and set in the center.
8. Enjoy!

Nutritional Info: Calories: 151 kcal ‖ Protein: 17.92 g ‖ Fat: 7.32 g ‖ Carbohydrates: 3.75 g

Zucchini Bread

Time To Prepare: ten minutes

Time to Cook: 60 minutes

Yield: Servings 16

Ingredients:

- ¼ teaspoon baking powder
- 1 cup canola oil
- 1 cup chopped pecans
- 1 cup raisins
- 1 tablespoon cinnamon
- 1 teaspoon baking soda
- 1 teaspoon salt
- 1½ cups 100% whole-wheat flour
- 1½ cups all-purpose flour
- 2 cups grated zucchini
- 2 cups sugar
- 3 eggs, beaten, or ¾ cup of egg substitute

Directions:

1. Preheat your oven to 350°F. Oil 2 loaf pans and save for later.

2. Put and mix the flour, salt, baking soda, baking powder, and cinnamon in a container.
3. Combine the eggs, oil, and sugar in a different container.
4. Put in the zucchini and dry ingredients alternately until fully blended into a smooth batter. Fold in the pecans and raisins and scrape the batter into the loaf pans.
5. Bake for 60 minutes, cool on a rack, and wrap when cool.

Nutritional Info: Calories: 396 ‖ Fat: 20 ‖ Protein: 5 g ‖ Sodium: 237 mg ‖ Fiber: 3 g ‖ Carbohydrates: 52 g

Zucchini Pancakes

Time To Prepare: fifteen minutes
Time to Cook: 6-10 min
Yield: Servings 8

Ingredients:

- ¼ cup fresh cilantro, chopped
- ¼ teaspoon cumin seeds
- ¼ teaspoon ground turmeric
- ¼ tsp cayenne
- ½ cup red onion, chopped finely
- ½ cup zucchini, shredded
- 1 cup chickpea flour
- 1 green chile, seeded and chopped finely
- 1½ cups water, divided
- Salt, to taste

Directions:

1. In a big container, put in flour and ¾ cup with the water and beat till smooth.
2. Put in remaining water and beat till a thin
3. Fold inside the onion, ginger, Serrano pepper, and cilantro.

4. Lightly, grease a substantial nonstick frying pan with oil and heat on medium-low heat.

5. Put in about ¼ cup of mixture and tilt the pan to spread it uniformly in the frying pan.

6. Cook for around 4-6 minutes.

7. Cautiously, alter the side and cook for roughly 2-4 minutes.

8. Repeat while using the rest of the mixture.

9. Serve with your desired topping.

Nutritional Info: Calories: 389 ‖ Fat: 13g ‖ Carbohydrates: 25g ‖ Fiber: 4g ‖ Protein: 21g

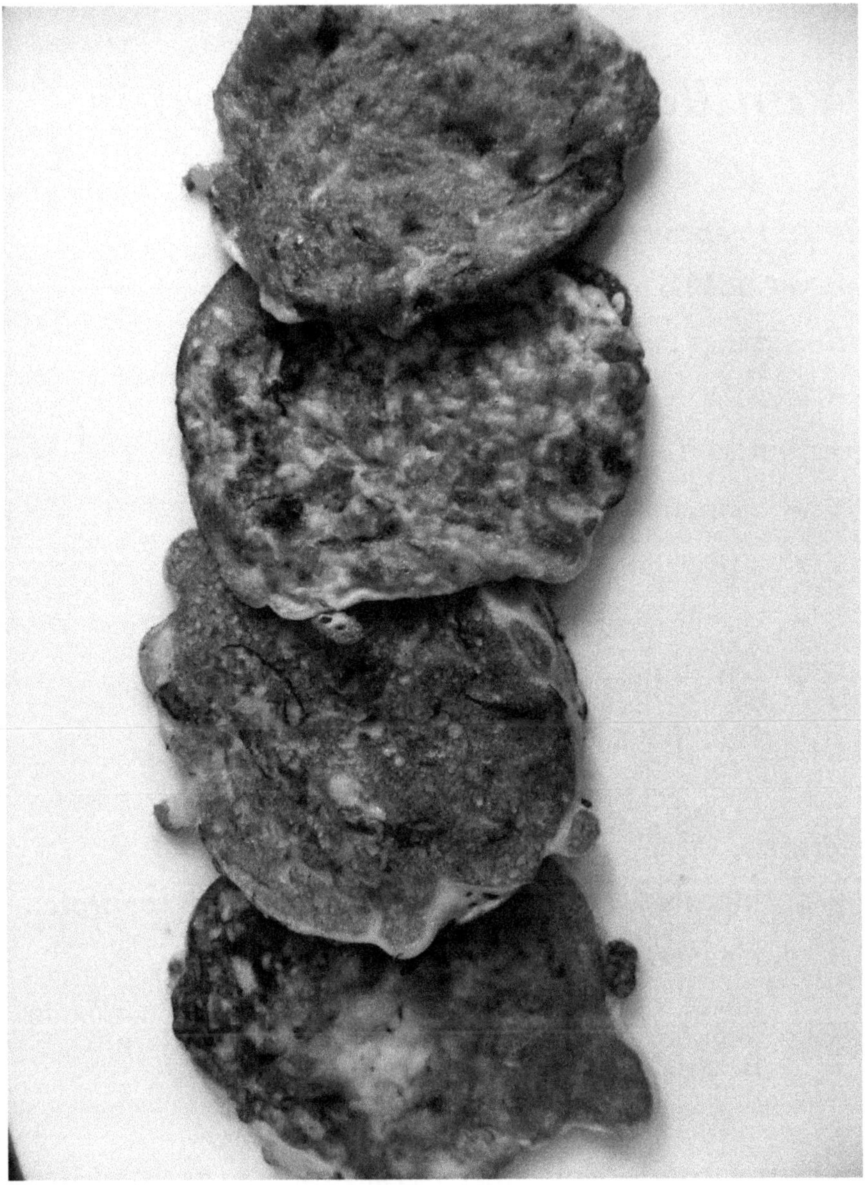

SMOOTHIES AND DRINKS

Vanilla Blueberry Smoothie

Time To Prepare: five minutes

Time to Cook: 0 minutes

Yield: Servings 1

Ingredients:

- 1 cup fresh blueberries
- 1 tbsp. flaxseed oil
- 2 cups hemp milk
- 2 tbsp. hemp protein powder
- Handful of ice/ 1 cup frozen blueberries

Directions:

1. Mix milk and fresh blueberries plus ice (or frozen blueberries) in a blender.
2. Blend for a minute, move to a glass, and mix in flaxseed oil.

Nutritional Info: Calories: 1041 kcal ‖ Protein: 35.21 g ‖ Fat: 41.04 g ‖ Carbohydrates: 140.4 g

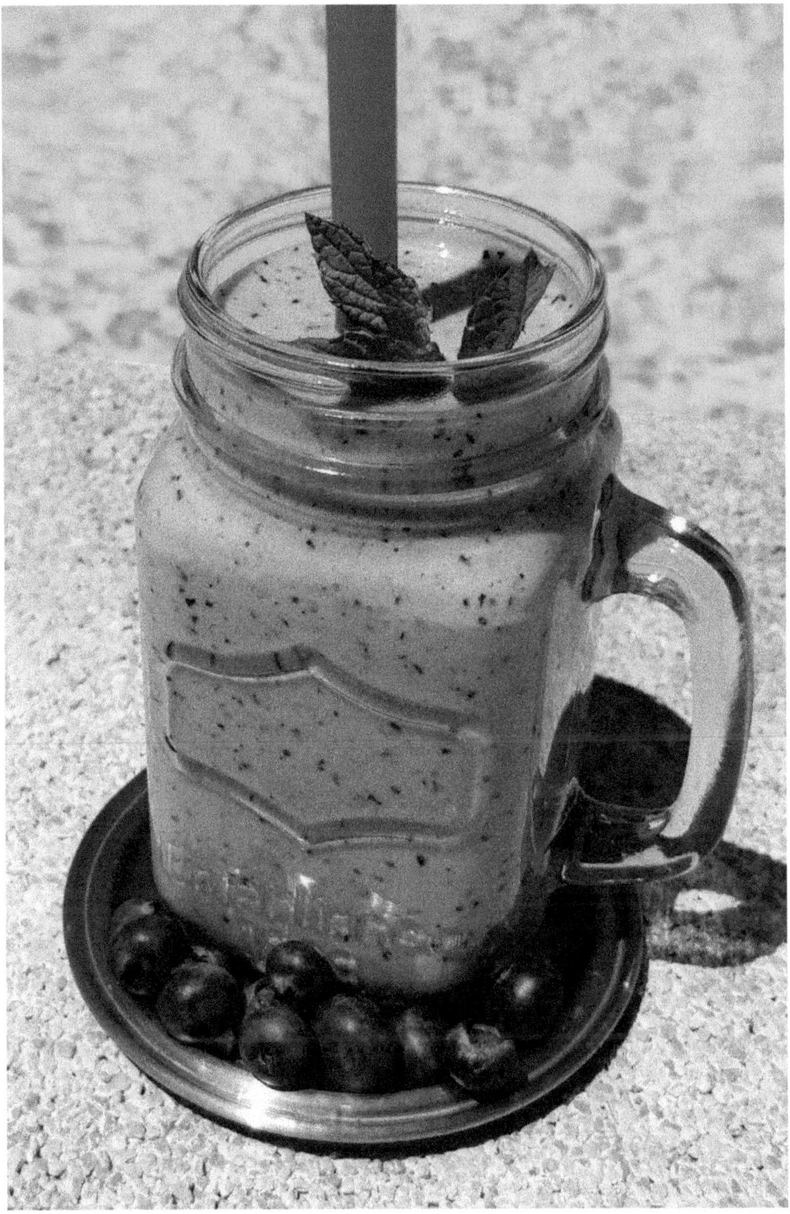

Vanilla Turmeric Orange Juice

Time To Prepare: five minutes

Time to Cook: 0 minutes

Yield: Servings 2

Ingredients:

- ½ teaspoon turmeric powder
- 1 teaspoon ground cinnamon
- 2 cups unsweetened almond milk
- 2 teaspoons vanilla extract
- 6 oranges, peeled, separated into segments, deseeded
- Pepper to taste

Directions:

1. Juice the oranges. Put in the remaining ingredients.
2. Pour into 2 glasses before you serve.

Nutritional Info: Calories: 223 kcal ‖ Protein: 11.47 g ‖ Fat: 11.79 g ‖ Carbohydrates: fifteen.9 g

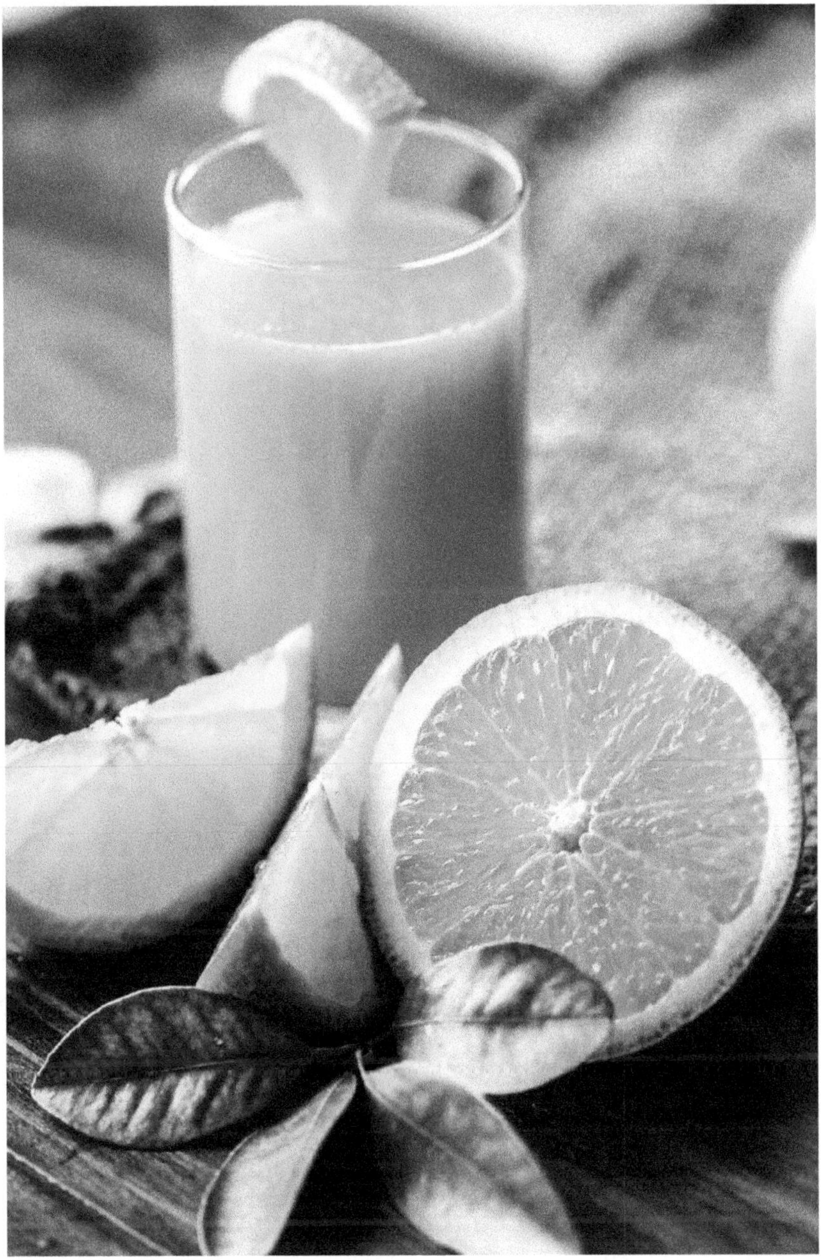

Voluptuous Vanilla Hot Drink

Time To Prepare: ten minutes

Time to Cook: 0 minutes

Yield: Servings 1

Ingredients:

- 1 scoop of hemp protein
- 1/2 Tbsp. ground cinnamon (or more to taste)
- 1/2 Tbsp. vanilla extract
- 3 cups unsweetened almond milk (or 1 1/2 cup full-fat coconut milk + 1 1/2 cups water)
- Stevia to taste

Directions:

1. Put the almond milk into a pitcher. Put ground cinnamon, hemp, vanilla extract in a small deep cooking pan on moderate to high heat. Heat until the pure liquid stevia is just melted and then pour the pure liquid stevia mixture into the pitcher.

2. Stir until the pure liquid stevia is well blended with the almond milk. Bring the pitcher in your refrigerator and let it cool for minimum two hours. Stir thoroughly before you serve.

Nutritional Info: Calories: 656 kcal ‖ Protein: 42.12 g ‖ Fat: 33.05 g ‖ Carbohydrates: 44.45 g

Wassail

Time To Prepare: five minutes

Time to Cook: ten minutes

Yield: Servings 4

Ingredients:

- ½ tsp nutmeg
- 1 inch peeled ginger
- 10 cloves
- 2 vanilla beans, split or 2 Tbsp pure vanilla extract
- 4 cups orange juice
- 5 cinnamon sticks
- 8 cups apple cider
- Zest and juice of 2 lemons

Directions:

1. Pour cider and orange juice in the instant pot.
2. Put cinnamon sticks, nutmeg piece, cloves, lemon zest, vanilla beans in the steamer basket.
3. If you didn't use vanilla beans, pour in vanilla extract. Put in lemon juice.
4. Secure the lid. Cook on HIGH pressure ten minutes.
5. When done, depressurize naturally.
6. Discard contents of the steamer basket.

7. Serve hot from the pot.

Nutritional Info: Calories: 221 ‖ Fat: 0g ‖ Carbohydrates: 42g ‖
Protein: 0g

White Hot Chocolate

Time To Prepare: five minutes

Time to Cook: six minutes

Yield: Servings 2

Ingredients:

- ¼ cup cocoa powder/butter
- 2 - 2½ Tbsp honey
- 2 tsp vanilla extract
- 3 cups coconut milk
- Pinch of sea salt

Directions:

1. Put in milk, cocoa powder/butter, honey, vanilla extract, and salt to the instant pot.
2. Secure the lid. Cook on LOW pressure six minutes.
3. Depressurize swiftly.
4. Use a hand blender to blend contents 25 seconds.
5. Serve hot.

Nutritional Info: Calories: 331 ‖ Fat: 14g ‖ Carbohydrates: 47g ‖ Protein: 4g

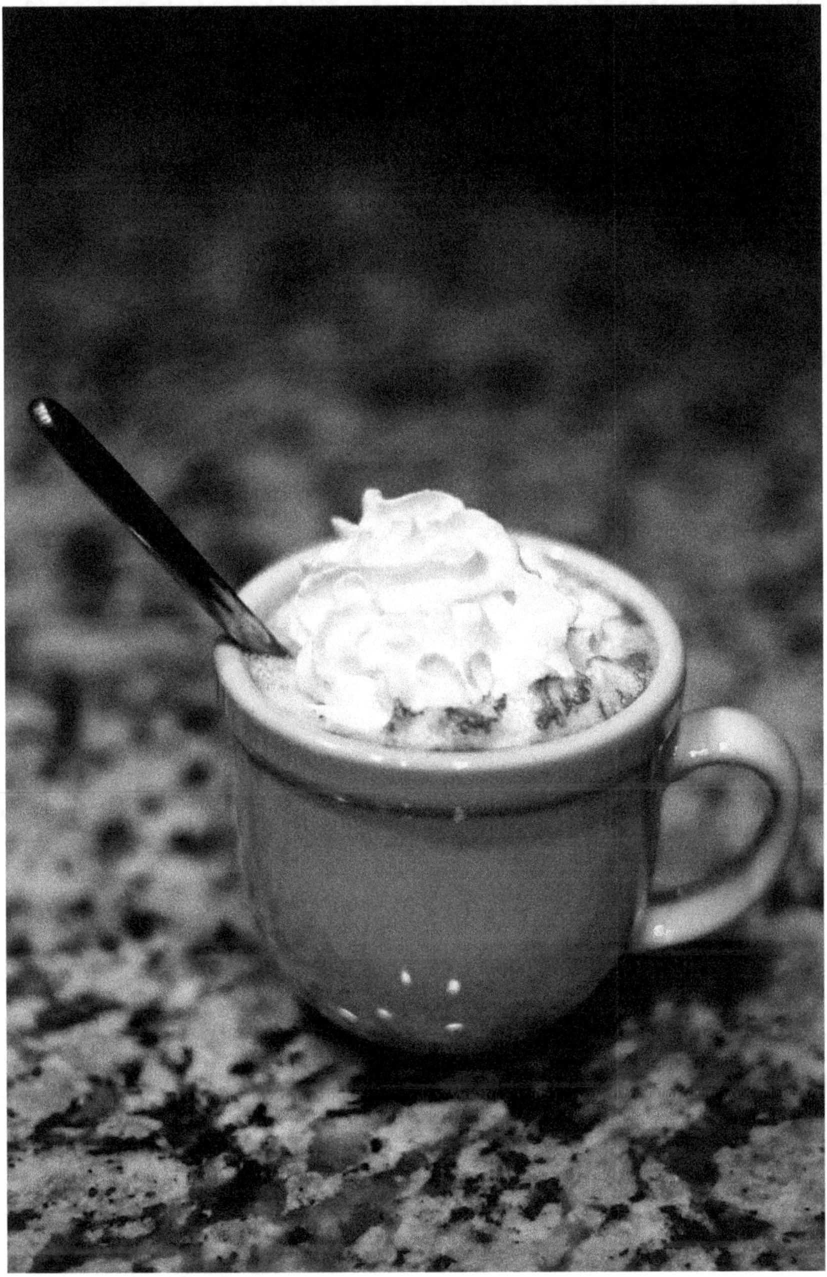

Wonderful Watermelon Drink

Time To Prepare: five minutes

Time to Cook: 0 minutes

Yield: Servings 2

Ingredients:

- 1 cup of coconut water
- 1 cup of watermelon chunks
- 1/2 cup of tart cherries
- 2 cups of frozen mixed berries
- 2 tbsp. of chia seeds

Directions:

1. Combine all ingredients in a blender or juicer then blend until pureed.
2. Serve instantly and enjoy!

Nutritional Info: Calories: 330 kcal ‖ Protein: 10.22 g ‖ Fat: 9.71 g ‖ Carbohydrates: 53.3 g

Zesty Citrus Smoothie

Time To Prepare: five minutes

Time to Cook: 0 minutes

Yield: Servings 1

Ingredients:

- 1 cup almond milk
- 1 med orange peeled, cleaned, and cut into sections
- 1 tbsp. flaxseed oil
- 2 tsp hemp protein powder
- half cup lemon juice
- Handful of ice

Directions:

1. Mix milk, lemon juice, orange, and ice in a blender.
2. Blend for a minute, move to a glass, and mix in flaxseed oil.

Nutritional Info: Calories: 427 kcal ‖ Protein: 17.5 g ‖ Fat: 28.88 g ‖ Carbohydrates: 24.96 g

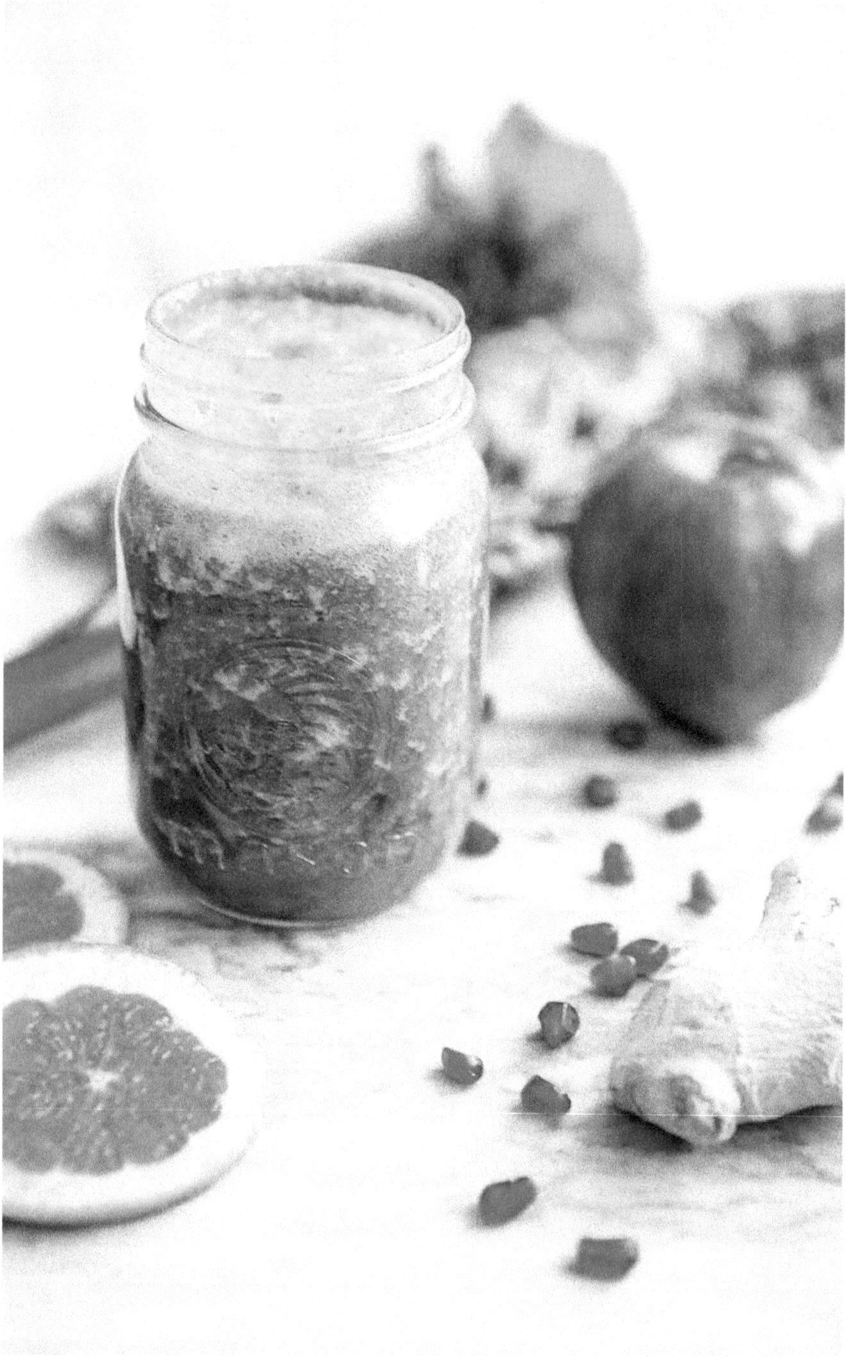

SIDES

Tender Farro

Time To Prepare: 8 minutes

Time to Cook: forty minutes

Yield: Servings 4

Ingredients:

- 1 cup farro
- 1 tablespoon almond butter
- 1 tablespoon dried dill
- 1 teaspoon salt
- 3 cups beef broth

Directions:

1. Put farro in the pan.
2. Put in beef broth, dried dill, and salt.
3. Close the lid and put the mixture to boil.
4. Then boil it for a little more than half an hour over the medium-low heat.
5. When the time is done, open the lid and put in almond butter.
6. Mix up the cooked farro well.

Nutritional Info: Calories 95 ‖ Fat: 3.3 ‖ Fiber: 1.3 ‖ Carbs: 10.1 ‖ Protein: 6.4

Thyme with Honey-Roasted Carrots

Time To Prepare: five minutes
Time to Cook: thirty minutes
Yield: Servings 4

Ingredients:

- ½ teaspoon of sea salt
- ½ teaspoon thyme, dried
- 1 tablespoon of honey
- 1/5 lb. carrots, with the tops
- 2 tablespoons of olive oil

Directions:

1. Preheat the oven to 425 degrees F.
2. Place parchment paper on your baking sheet.
3. Toss your carrots with honey, oil, thyme, and salt. Coat well.
4. Keep in a single layer. Bake in the oven for half an hour
5. Allow to cool before you serve.

Nutritional Info: Calories 85 ‖ Carbohydrates: 6g ‖ Cholesterol: 0mg ‖ Total Fat: 8g ‖ Protein: 1g ‖ Sugar: 6g ‖ Fiber: 1g ‖ Sodium: 244mg

Tomato Bulgur

Time To Prepare: seven minutes

Time to Cook: twenty minutes

Yield: Servings 2

Ingredients:

- ½ cup bulgur
- ½ white onion, diced
- 1 ½ cup chicken stock
- 1 teaspoon tomato paste
- 2 tablespoons coconut oil

Directions:

1. Toss coconut oil in the pan and melt it.
2. Put in diced onion and roast it until light brown.
3. Then put in bulgur and stir thoroughly.
4. Cook bulgur in coconut oil for about three minutes.
5. Then put in tomato paste and mix up bulgur until homogenous.
6. Put in chicken stock.
7. Close the lid and cook bulgur for fifteen minutes over the moderate heat.
8. The cooked bulgur should soak all liquid.

Nutritional Info: Calories 257 ‖ Fat: 14.5 ‖ Fiber: 7.1 ‖ Carbs: 30.2 ‖ Protein: 5.2

Wheatberry Salad

Time To Prepare: ten minutes

Time to Cook: 50 minutes

Yield: Servings 2

Ingredients:

- ¼ cup fresh parsley, chopped
- ¼ cup of wheat berries
- 1 cup of water
- 1 tablespoon canola oil
- 1 tablespoon chives, chopped
- 1 teaspoon chili flakes
- 1 teaspoon salt
- 2 oz. pomegranate seeds
- 2 tablespoons walnuts, chopped

Directions:

1. Put wheat berries and water in the pan.
2. Put in salt and simmer the ingredients for about fifty minutes over the moderate heat.
3. In the meantime, mix up together walnuts, chives, parsley, pomegranate seeds, and chili flakes.

4. When the wheatberry is cooked, move it in the walnut mixture.

5. Put in canola oil and mix up the salad well.

Nutritional Info: Calories 160 ‖ Fat: 11.8 ‖ Fiber: 1.2 ‖ Carbs: 12 ‖ Protein: 3.4

SAUCES AND DRESSINGS

Tomato and Mushroom Sauce

Time To Prepare: ten minutes
Time to Cook: 0 minutes
Yield: Servings 2-4

Ingredients:

- ½ cup of water
- 1 moderate-sized leek, chopped
- 2 moderate-sized carrots, chopped
- 2 stalks of celery, chopped
- 2 tsp of dried oregano
- 4 cloves of garlic, crushed
- 450g of button mushrooms, diced
- 5 tbsp. of coconut milk
- 680g of unsalted tomato puree
- Black pepper, seasoning
- Some sea salt, seasoning

Directions:

1. In a big frying pan, place a few tablespoons of water and heat on moderate heat. Once it sizzles, put in in

the mushrooms and Sautee for approximately five minutes, stir once in a while.

2. Next, put in in the leek, carrots, and celery. Stir thoroughly and cook for approximately five minutes or until the vegetables are soft. Put in more water if required.

3. Mix in the tomato puree with ½ cup of water and dried oregano. Bring to its boiling point and then decrease the heat to allow it to simmer for approximately fifteen minutes.

4. Remove from heat and mix in the garlic, coconut milk, and salt and pepper to taste.

5. Put in an airtight container, then store for maximum four days in your fridge or freeze for maximum 1 month. Serve with a pasta.

Nutritional Info: ‖ Calories: 467 kcal ‖ Protein: 16.91 g ‖ Fat: 3.81 g ‖ Carbohydrates: 109.68 g

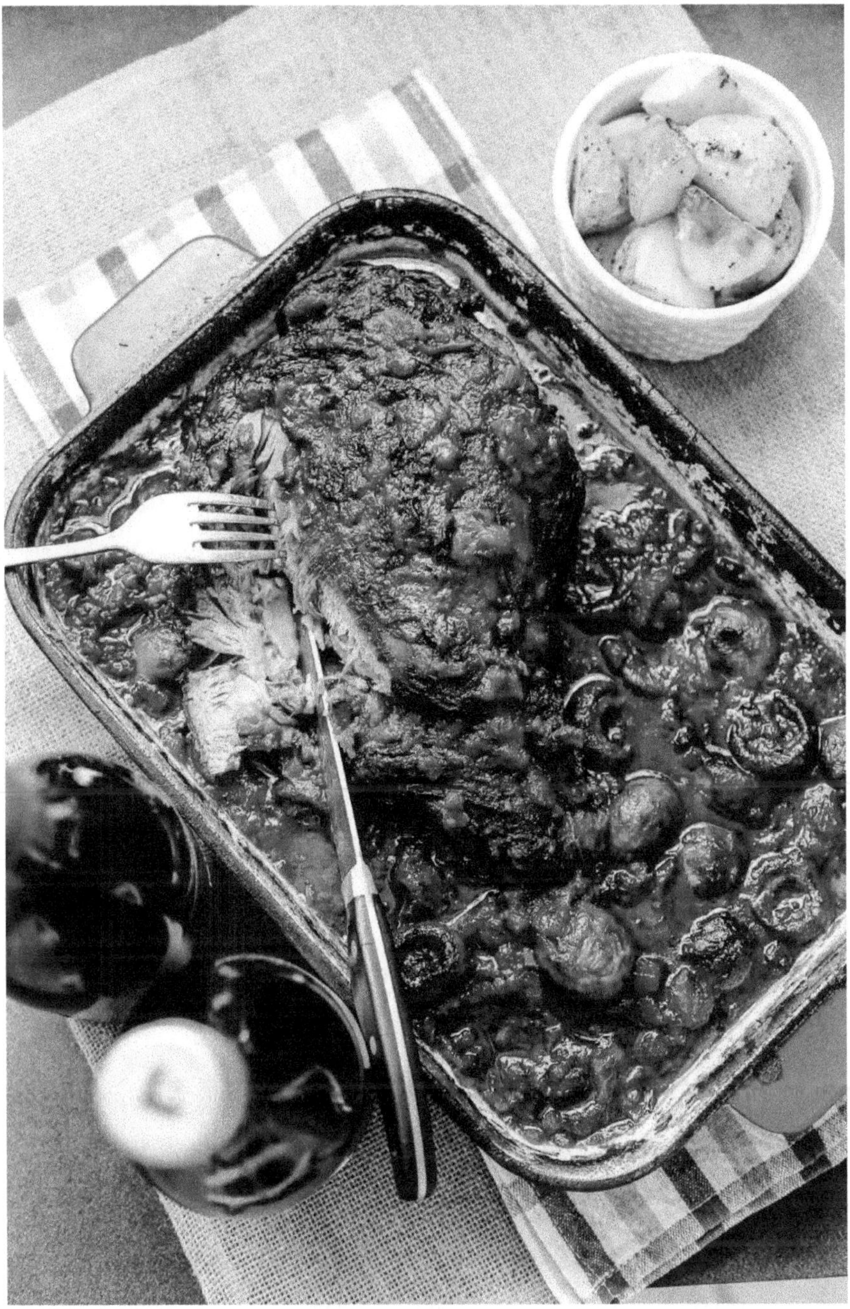

SNACKS

Sweet Potato Muffins

Time To Prepare: fifteen minutes
Time to Cook: 20-twenty-five minutes
Yield: Servings 12

Ingredients:

- ¼ Cup Almond Butter
- ¼ Teaspoon Sea Salt
- ½ Teaspoon Baking Soda
- 1 ½ Cups Rolled Oats
- 1 Cup Almond Milk
- 1 Cup Sweet Potato, Cooked & Pureed
- 1 Egg
- 1 Teaspoon Baking Powder
- 1 Teaspoon Ground Cinnamon
- 1 Teaspoon Vanilla Extract, Pure
- 1/3 Cup Coconut Sugar
- 2 Tablespoons Olive Oil

Directions:

1. Begin by heating the oven to 375.

2. Coat your muffin tin with liners, and get out a food processor.

3. Pulse your oats until it forms a course flour. Move it to a small container before setting it to the side.

4. Put in all of your ingredients apart from for the oat flour, blending until the desired smoothness is achieved.

5. Slowly put in in your oat flour, pulsing until it's well blended.

6. Cut between your cupcake liners, and bake for about twenty minutes. Let them cool for minimum five minutes before you serve.

Nutritional Info: ‖ Calories: 143 ‖ Protein: 4 Grams ‖ Fat: 7 Grams ‖ Carbohydrates: 12 Grams

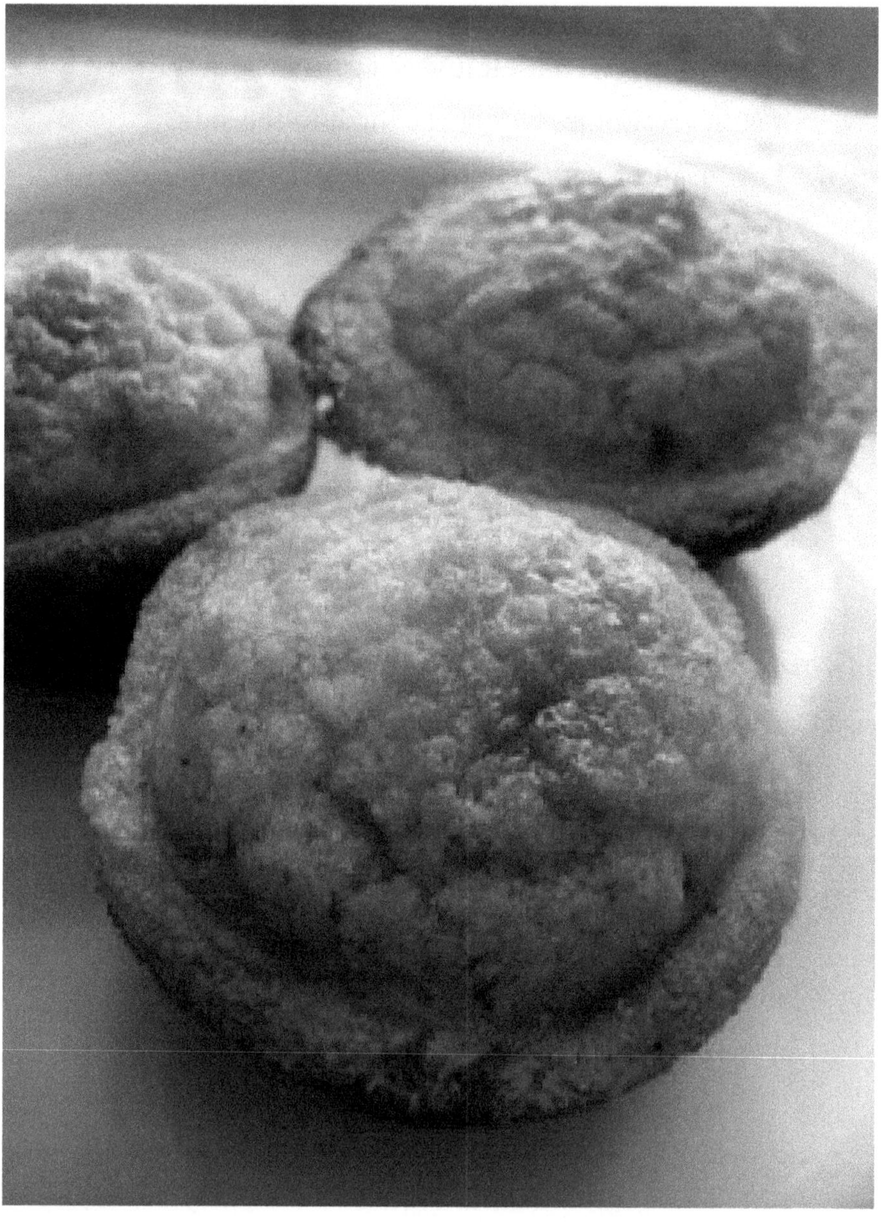

Sweet Sunup Seeds

Time To Prepare: five minutes
Time to Cook: 60 minutes
Yield: Servings 8

Ingredients:

- ¼-cup pure maple syrup
- ¼-cup sunflower oil
- ¼-sesame seeds
- ⅓ -cup honey
- ½-cup flaxseed
- 1-cup dried cranberries
- 1-cup raw pumpkin seeds
- 1-tsp vanilla extract
- 3-tsp cinnamon
- 4-cups rolled oats

Directions:

1. Preheat your oven to 350°F. Prepare two units of baking sheets by lining them using parchment paper.
2. In a large-sized mixing container, mix the rolled oats, pumpkin seeds, flaxseed, sesame seeds, and cinnamon. Mix gently until meticulously blended.

3. Pour all the liquid ingredients into the mixture and stir until mixed well.
4. On the baking sheets, spread the mixture uniformly. Place the sheets in your oven. Cook for minimum an hour. While baking, stir the mixture every quarter of an hour to achieve uniform color on its surfaces.
5. Take away the sheets from the oven. Allow cooling completely. Put in the cup of dried cranberries, and mix thoroughly.
6. Store the granola in an airtight container to maintain its freshness and crunchiness.

Nutritional Info: ‖ Calories: 189 ‖ Fat: 6.3g ‖ Protein: 9.4g ‖ Sodium: 5mg ‖ Total Carbohydrates: 27.6g ‖ Fiber: 4g ‖ Net Carbohydrates: 23.6g

Tangy Turmeric Flavored Florets

Time To Prepare: ten minutes

Time to Cook: 55 minutes

Yield: Servings 1

Ingredients:

- 1-head cauliflower, chopped into florets
- 1-Tbsp olive oil
- 1-Tbsp turmeric
- A dash of salt
- A pinch of cumin

Directions:

1. Set the oven to 400°F.
2. Combine all ingredients in a baking pan. Mix thoroughly until meticulously blended.
3. Cover the pan using foil. Roast for forty minutes. Take away the foil cover and roast additionally for fifteen minutes.

Nutritional Info: ‖ Calories: 90 ‖ Fat: 3g ‖ Protein: 4.5g ‖ Sodium: 87mg ‖ Total Carbohydrates: 16.2g ‖ Fiber: 5g ‖ Net Carbohydrates: 11.2g

Toasted Pumpkin Seeds

Time To Prepare: five minutes

Time to Cook: thirty minutes

Yield: Servings 2-4

Ingredients:

- ½ teaspoon extra virgin olive oil
- 1 teaspoon salt
- 1 to 2 cups pumpkin seeds
- Sea salt
- Water

Directions:

1. Put seeds in a deep cooking pan and cover with water. Put in salt.
2. Bring it to its boiling point and boil for about ten minutes.
3. Simmer uncovered for ten more minutes. This makes the seeds very crunchy when baked. Drain the seeds and pat dry using a paper towel.
4. Coat a baking sheet using parchment paper and spread out the seeds in a single layer.
5. Sprinkle with salt, then bake in an oven at 325F for minimum ten minutes, stirring midway through.

6. Cool, then store in an airtight container.

Nutritional Info: ‖ Calories: 192 kcal ‖ Protein: 10.41 g ‖ Fat: 16.23 g ‖ Carbohydrates: 4.34 g

Tofu Pudding

Time To Prepare: ten minutes
Time to Cook: 0 minutes
Yield: Servings 4

Ingredients:

- 1 cup strawberries
- 1 teaspoon honey
- 1 teaspoon pumpkin pie spice
- 1 teaspoon vanilla
- 12 ounces silken tofu, softened and well-drained
- 2 scoops of Protein powder
- 3/4 cup blueberries
- 4 almonds
- Fresh mint leaves

Directions:

1. Combine the tofu and Protein powder in a blender until thoroughly combincd.
2. Put in the blueberries, strawberries, honey, pumpkin pie spice, and vanilla. Blend until the desired smoothness is achieved.

3. Cover and put on the refrigerator to chill for minimum 2 hours.
4. Ladle into four dessert bowls and top with an almond and a mint leaf before you serve.

Nutritional Info: ‖ Calories: 371 kcal ‖ Protein: 23.31 g ‖ Fat: 21.1 g ‖ Carbohydrates: 27.17 g

Turmeric Chickpea Cakes

Time To Prepare: twenty minutes

Time to Cook: thirty minutes

Yield: Servings 8

Ingredients:

- ½ cup fresh parsley, minced
- 1 teaspoon cayenne pepper, to taste (not necessary)
- 1 teaspoon salt or to taste
- 2 cans (15oz.) chickpeas, washed, drained
- 2 small onions, minced
- 2 teaspoons turmeric powder
- 4 cloves garlic, minced
- 4 tablespoons cornstarch
- 8-10 tablespoons chickpea flour
- Avocado dipping sauce to serve
- Freshly ground pepper to taste
- Grapeseed oil to fry

Directions:

1. Put a frying pan on moderate heat. Put in a little oil. When the oil is heated, put onion and garlic and sauté

until translucent. Remove the heat and cool to room temperature.

2. Put in chickpeas into the food processor container and pulse until very finely chopped.

3. Put in the onion mixture, salt, pepper, cayenne pepper, and turmeric powder and pulse again until well blended.

4. Move into a container. Put in parsley and mix thoroughly.

5. Make small balls of the mixture (of approximately 1 inch diameter) and mould into patties. Put chickpea flour on a plate.

6. Put a nonstick pan on moderate heat. Put in a little oil and swirl the pan so that the oil spreads.

7. Immerse the patties in the chickpea flour and place a few on the pan. Cook in batches.

8. Cook until the underside is golden brown. Flip then cook the other side till it's golden brown.

9. Repeat steps 6-8 to fry the rest of the patties.

10. Serve with avocado dipping sauce.

Nutritional Info: ‖ Calories: 154 kcal ‖ Protein: 7.32 g ‖ Fat: 2.85 g ‖ Carbohydrates: 25.43 g

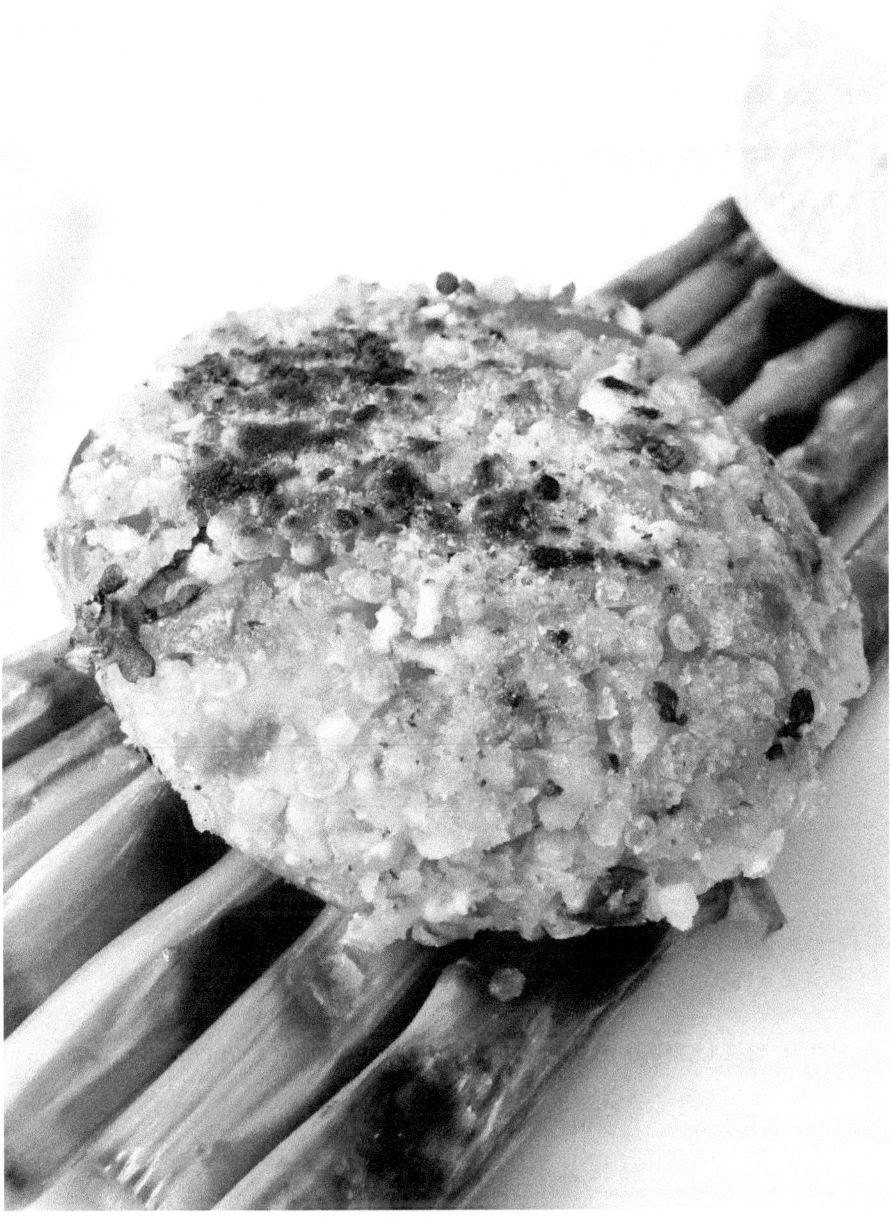

Turmeric Coconut Flour Muffins

Time To Prepare: five minutes

Time to Cook: twenty-five minutes

Yield: Servings 8

Ingredients:

- ½ cup Unsweetened coconut milk
- ½ tsp. Baking soda
- ½ tsp. Ginger powder
- ¾ cup & 2 tbsp. Coconut flour
- 1 tsp. Vanilla extract
- 1/3 cup Maple syrup
- 2 tsp. Turmeric
- 6 big Whole eggs
- Pepper and salt

Directions:

1. Preheat your oven to 350°F.
2. Coat 8 muffin tins with 8 muffin liners.
3. Whisk eggs, maple syrup, milk, and vanilla extract in a mixing container until the egg begins to make bubbles.

4. In a different container, combine the coconut flour, turmeric powder, pepper, baking soda, ginger powder, and salt.
5. Place the dry mixture into the wet mixture then stir until it's all mixed and thick.
6. Ladle out the batter into prepared muffin tins.
7. Leave to bake for about twenty-five minutes or until it looked golden.
8. Allow the muffins cool for a couple of minutes before transferring them to a rack.

Nutritional Info: ‖ Calories: 143 kcal ‖ Protein: 6.18 g ‖ Fat: 8 g ‖ Carbohydrates: 11.8 g

Turmeric Gummies

Time To Prepare: five minutes

Time to Cook: 4 hours and ten minutes

Yield: Servings 4

Ingredients:

- ¼ tsp. Ground pepper
- 1 tsp. Ground turmeric
- 3 ½ cups Water
- 6 tbsp. Maple syrup
- 8 tbsp. Unflavored gelatin powder

Directions:

1. Combine the ground turmeric, maple syrup, and water in a pot set on moderate heat. Stir continuously for five minutes before removing from heat and pouring in the gelatin powder. Stir using a wooden spoon to dissolve the gelatin.

2. Put back the pan on the heat and stir for another two minutes.

3. Remove the heat and take the mixture to a deep container that you will seal using plastic wrapimmediately after.

4. Place in your fridge the mixture for approximately 4 hours.

5. It must be firm now, cut it into little squares, and serve or store.

Nutritional Info: ‖ Calories: 123 kcal ‖ Protein: 2.15 g ‖ Fat: 1.56 g ‖ Carbohydrates: 25.67 g

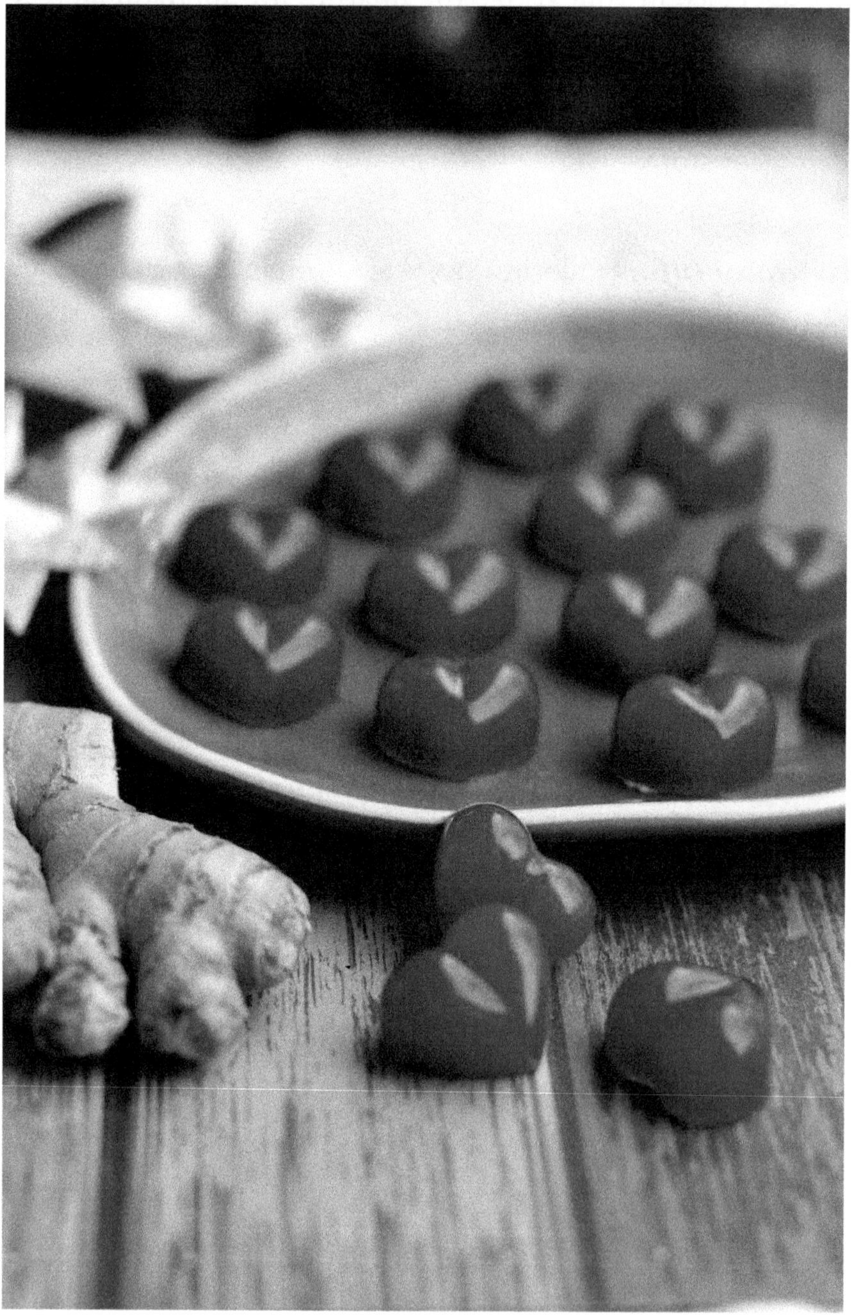

SOUPS AND STEWS

Tomato And Basil Soup

Time To Prepare: five minutes

Time to Cook: fifteen minutes

Yield: Servings 4

Ingredients:

- ¼ cup chopped fresh basil leaves
- ¼ cup heavy whipping cream
- 1 (14.5-ounce / 411-g) can diced tomatoes
- 2 ounces (57 g) cream cheese
- 4 tablespoons butter
- From the cupboard:
- Salt and freshly ground black pepper, to taste

Directions:

1. Position the diced tomatoes in a food processor. Process until the desired smoothness is achieved.
2. Melt the butter in a deep cooking pan on moderate heat. Put in the tomato purée, cream, and cheese. Cook for about ten minutes or until well blended. Keep stirring during the cooking.

76

3. Drizzle with chopped basil leaves, salt, and black pepper. Keep cooking for another five minutes or until the desired smoothness is achieved and the soup has become thick. Stir continuously.
4. Ladle the soup into a big container and serve warm.

Nutritional Info: calories: 238 ‖ total fat: 22.1g ‖ total carbs: 8.9g ‖ fiber: 2.1g ‖ net carbs: 6.8g ‖ protein: 3.1g

Tomato Bisque Soup

Time To Prepare: ten minutes

Time to Cook: forty minutes

Yield: Servings 6

Ingredients:

- 1 cup heavy cream
- 1 teaspoon freshly chopped thyme
- 2 tablespoons butter
- 3 cloves garlic, chopped
- 3 cups canned whole, peeled tomatoes
- 4 cups chicken broth
- Salt & black pepper, to taste

Directions:

1. Put in the butter to the bottom of a stockpot.
2. Put in in all the rest of the ingredients minus the heavy cream. Bring to its boiling point, and then simmer for forty minutes.
3. Warm the heavy cream, and then mix into the soup.

Nutritional Info: Calories: 144 ‖ Carbohydrates: 4g ‖ Fiber: 1g Net ‖ Carbohydrates: 3g ‖ Fat: 12g ‖ Protein: 4g

Turkey Meatball Soup

Time To Prepare: fifteen minutes

Time to Cook: fifteen minutes

Yield: Servings 6

Ingredients:

For the Meatballs:

- ¼ teaspoon red pepper flakes
- ½ teaspoon dried oregano
- ½ teaspoon salt
- 1 pound ground turkey
- 1 tablespoon Dijon mustard
- 1 tablespoon ghee
- 1 teaspoon dried basil
- 1 teaspoon garlic powder
- Freshly ground black pepper

For the Soup:

- ½ teaspoon dried thyme
- 1 bay leaf
- 1 medium white onion, diced
- 2 carrots, diced
- 2 cups shredded kale leaves, stemmed and meticulously washed

- 2 garlic cloves, minced
- 6 cups vegetable broth

Directions:
To make the Meatballs:

1. In a moderate-sized container, put the turkey, mustard, basil, garlic powder, oregano, salt, and red pepper flakes, and flavor with pepper. With your hands, combine the ingredients until they are well blended.

2. Put in the ghee to a stockpot on moderate to high heat. Roll the meat mixture into 1-inch balls and layer across the bottom of the pot. Cook for minimum 2 minutes per side, until almost thoroughly cooked. Move the meatballs to a plate.

To make the Soup:

1. To the stockpot, put in the onion, carrots, garlic, and thyme. Cook for approximately 2 minutes, slowly stirring, until the onions are translucent.

2. Put in the broth, kale, bay leaf, and meatballs. Put to a simmer, lessen the heat to moderate-low and simmer for approximately fifteen minutes until the meatballs are thoroughly cooked, and the kale has tenderized. Remove and discard the bay leaf. Serve hot.

Nutritional Info: Calories: 259 ‖ Total Fat: 14g ‖ Saturated Fat: 5g ‖ Cholesterol: 88mg ‖ Carbohydrates: 9g ‖ Fiber: 2g ‖ Protein: 26g

Tuscan Style Soup

Time To Prepare: three minutes
Time to Cook: five minutes
Yield: Servings 4

Ingredients:

- ½ cup leeks, cut
- 1 carrot, trimmed and grated
- 1 zucchini, shredded
- 1/4 teaspoon ground black pepper
- 2 cups broth, if possible homemade
- 2 cups water
- 2 garlic cloves, minced
- 2 tablespoons butter, melted
- 4 cups broccoli rabe, broken into pieces
- Sea salt, to taste

Directions:

1. Push the "Sauté" button to heat up your Instant Pot; now, melt the butter. Cook the leeks for approximately 2 minutes or until tender.
2. Put in minced garlic and cook an additional 40 seconds.

3. Put in the rest of the ingredients. Secure the lid.

4. "Manual" mode and Low pressure; cook for about three minutes. Once cooking is complete, use a quick pressure release; cautiously remove the lid. Enjoy!

Nutritional Info: 95 Calories ‖ 6.7g Fat ‖ 5.2g Total Carbs ‖ 4.2g Protein ‖ 1.4g Sugars

Vegetable Beef Soup

Time To Prepare: ten minutes

Time to Cook: 4-6 hours

Yield: Servings 6

Ingredients:

- ½ cup diced tomatoes
- 1 pound lean ground beef
- 1 teaspoon freshly chopped rosemary
- 1 teaspoon freshly chopped thyme
- 1 yellow onion, chopped
- 1 zucchini, diced
- 2 cloves garlic, chopped
- 2 stalks celery, chopped
- 4 cups beef broth
- Salt & pepper, to taste

Directions:

1. Put in all the ingredients to a slow cooker and cook on high for four to 6 hours.
2. Stir thoroughly before you serve.

Nutritional Info: Calories: 185 ‖ Carbohydrates: 5g ‖ Fiber: 1g
Net ‖ Carbohydrates: 4g ‖ Fat: 6g ‖ Protein: 7g

Vegetarian Garlic, Tomato & Onion Soup

Time To Prepare: fifteen minutes
Time to Cook: thirty minutes
Yield: Servings 6

Ingredients:

- ½ cup full-fat unsweetened coconut milk
- 1 bay leaf
- 1 teaspoon Italian seasoning
- 1 yellow onion, chopped
- 1½ cups canned diced tomatoes
- 3 cloves garlic, chopped
- 6 cups vegetable broth
- Fresh basil, for serving
- Pinch of salt & pepper, to taste

Directions:

1. Put in all the ingredients minus the coconut milk and fresh basil to a stockpot on moderate heat and bring to its boiling point. Reduce to a simmer and cook for half an hour

2. Take away the bay leaf, and then use an immersion blender to combine the soup until the desired smoothness is achieved. Mix in the coconut milk.

3. Decorate using fresh basil before you serve.

Nutritional Info: Calories: 104 ‖ Carbohydrates: 6g ‖ Fiber: 1g Net ‖ Carbohydrates: 5g ‖ Fat: 7g ‖ Protein: 6g

Wedding Soup

Time To Prepare: fifteen minutes

Time to Cook: 60 minutes

Yield: Servings 6

Ingredients:

- ¼ bunch fresh parsley, chopped
- ¾ pound lean ground beef
- 1 cup rough chopped fresh spinach with stems removed
- 1 egg or ¼ cup egg substitute
- 1 yellow onion, chopped
- 2 quarts Rich Poultry Stock or low-sodium canned chicken stock
- 2 sprigs fresh basil, chopped
- 3 cloves garlic, minced
- 3 slices Italian bread, toasted
- 3 sprigs fresh oregano, chopped
- 4 ounces fresh grated Parmesan cheese
- Freshly cracked black pepper, to taste

Directions:

1. Preheat your oven to 375°F.

2. Wet the toasted Italian bread with water, then squeeze out all the liquid.

3. In a big container, combine the bread, beef, egg, onion, garlic, parsley, oregano, basil, pepper, and half of the Parmesan. Form the mixture into 1- to two-inch balls; put in a baking dish and cook for twenty minutes to half an hour. Take off from the oven and drain using paper towels.

4. Steam the spinach firm to the bite. In a big stockpot, mix the stock, spinach, and meatballs; simmer for half an hour

5. Ladle the soup into serving bowls then top with the rest of the cheese

Nutritional Info: Calories: 245 ‖ Fat: 10 g ‖ Protein: 26 g ‖ Sodium: 1,021 mg ‖ Fiber: 0.5 g ‖ Carbohydrates: 9 g

White Velvet Cauliflower Soup

Time To Prepare: ten minutes

Time to Cook: twenty minutes

Yield: Servings 6

Ingredients:

- 1 head cauliflower, chopped into 1-inch pieces
- 1 small celery root, peeled, cut into 1-inch pieces
- 1 small white onion, diced
- 1 tbsp. avocado oil
- 2 scallions, cut
- 2 tbsp. ghee
- 3 garlic cloves, minced
- 4 cups vegetable broth

Directions:

1. In a huge soup pot on moderate heat, heat the avocado oil.
2. Place the onion and garlic, and sauté for five minutes.
3. Place the celery root and cauliflower.
4. Raise the heat to moderate-high, then continue to sauté for minimum five minutes, or until the cauliflower starts to brown and caramelize the sides.

5. Mix in the broth and ghee and place it to its boiling point. Lessen the heat to moderate-low and simmer for about ten minutes. Take away the pot from the heat.

6. Use an immersion blender to or in batches in a standard blender, purée the soup until creamy. Serve instantly, sprinkled with the scallions.

Nutritional Info: Calories: 183 ‖ Total Fat: 8g ‖ Saturated Fat: 3g ‖ Cholesterol: 0mg ‖ Carbohydrates: 10g ‖ Fiber: 3g ‖ Protein: 9g

Wholesome Cabbage Soup

Time To Prepare: two minutes

Time to Cook: 8 minutes

Yield: Servings 4

Ingredients:

- ½ pound Capocollo, chopped
- ½ teaspoon cayenne pepper
- 1 bay leaf
- 1 celery stalk, chopped
- 1 cup tomatoes, puréed
- 1 cup water
- 1 onion, chopped
- 1 parsnip, chopped
- 1 pound cabbage, cut into wedges
- 2 cups broth, if possible homemade
- Coarse sea salt and ground black pepper, to your preference

Directions:

1. Put in all of the above ingredients to your Instant Pot.
2. Secure the lid. Choose "Manual" mode and High pressure; cook for about three minutes. Once cooking

is complete, use a quick pressure release; cautiously remove the lid.

3. Ladle into four soup bowls and serve hot. Enjoy!

Nutritional Info: 258 Calories ‖ 20.4g Fat ‖ 6g Total Carbs ‖ 9.9g Protein ‖ 3.6g Sugars

Zesty Broccoli Soup

Time To Prepare: ten minutes

Time to Cook: twenty minutes

Yield: Servings 4

Ingredients:

- ½ teaspoon freshly squeezed lemon juice
- ½ teaspoon lemon zest
- ½ teaspoon salt
- 1 carrot, chopped
- 1 celery stalk, diced
- 1 head broccoli, roughly chopped
- 1 medium white onion, diced
- 1 tablespoon ghee
- 3 cups vegetable broth
- 3 garlic cloves, minced
- Freshly ground black pepper

Directions:

1. In a huge soup pot on moderate heat, melt the ghee.
2. Place the onion and garlic, and sauté for five minutes.
3. Put in the broccoli, carrot, and celery, and sauté for a couple of minutes.

4. Mix in the broth, salt, lemon juice, and lemon zest, and flavor with pepper. Heat to a simmer, and cook for minimum ten minutes. Serve instantly.

Nutritional Info: Calories: 80 ‖ Total Fat: 4g ‖ Saturated Fat: 2g ‖ Cholesterol: 0mg ‖ Carbohydrates: 10g ‖ Fiber: 3g ‖ Protein: 2g

Zucchini And Chicken Broth

Time To Prepare: twenty minutes

Time to Cook: twenty minutes

Yield: Servings 2

Ingredients:

- ¾ cup coconut milk
- 1 big zucchini, thinly cut
- 1 pound (454 g) boneless, skinless chicken breasts, cut into little pieces
- 1 tablespoon fresh parsley or fresh cilantro, finely chopped
- 2 cups water
- 2 garlic cloves, minced
- 2 tablespoons olive oil, divided
- 2 white onions, finely chopped
- 3 tablespoons green curry paste
- Salt and ground black pepper, to taste

Directions:

1. Sprinkle 1 tablespoon of olive oil in a deep cooking pan and warm on moderate heat.

2. Reduce the heat and cook the onions and garlic in the deep cooking pan using low heat for three to four minutes until translucent.

3. Then put the curry paste, coconut milk, parsley and water into the deep cooking pan. Bring them to a simmer for about three minutes.

4. Put in the chicken pieces and simmer for another six minutes until the chicken is thoroughly cooked.

5. In the meantime, warm the rest of the olive oil in a nonstick frying pan, then sauté the zucchini in the frying pan for about three minutes. Drizzle with salt and ground black pepper and sauté for another two minutes until tender.

6. Put in the cooked zucchini into the chicken broth and serve warm.

Nutritional Info: calories: 790 ‖ total fat: 54g ‖ net carbs: 18g ‖ fiber: 5g ‖ protein: 54g

DESSERTS

Tropical Fruit Crisp

Time To Prepare: ten minutes

Time to Cook: fifteen minutes

Yield: Servings 6

Ingredients:

For the Filling:

- 1 big mango (cut into chunks)
- 1 big pineapple (cut into chunks)
- 1/8 teaspoon of ground cinnamon
- 1/8 teaspoon of ground ginger
- 2 tablespoons of coconut oil
- 2 tablespoons of coconut sugar

For the Topping:

- ¾ cup of almonds
- ½ teaspoon of ground allspice
- ½ teaspoon of ground cinnamon
- ½ teaspoon of ground ginger
- 1/3 cup of unsweetened coconut, shredded

Directions:

1. Preheat your oven to 375 degrees F.

2. To make the filling: melt the coconut oil in a pan on medium-low heat and cook the coconut sugar for a couple of minutes while stirring.

3. Put in the rest of the ingredients then cook for minimum five minutes. Stir.

4. Take away the contents from heat and move it to a baking dish.

5. For the topping: Combine all ingredients in a mixer and pulse until a coarse meal forms.

6. Put the topping over the filling.

7. Bake for minimum fifteen minutes or until the top becomes golden brown.

Nutritional Info: ‖ Calories: 265 ‖ Fat: 12.4g ‖ Carbohydrates: 38g ‖ Sugar: 23.3g ‖ Protein: 4.3g ‖ Sodium: 17mg

Tropical Popsicles

Time To Prepare: 10 Minutes

Time to Cook*:* 10 Minutes

Yield: Servings 6

Ingredients:

- ½ tsp. Black Pepper
- 2 Kiwi, cut
- 2 tbsp. Coconut Oil
- 2 tsp. Turmeric
- 3 cups Pineapple, chopped

Directions:

1. First, place all the ingredients needed to make the popsicles excluding the kiwi in a high-speed blender for a couple of minutes or until you get a smooth mixture.
2. After this, pour the smoothie into the popsicle molds.
3. Next, insert the kiwi slices into the molds and then put the frames in the freezer until set.
4. Tip: If you desire texture, you can blend it less.

Nutritional Info: ‖ Calories: 101 Kcal ‖ Protein: 0.5g ‖ Carbohydrates: 15g ‖ Fat:4g

Turmeric Milkshake

Time To Prepare: five minutes

Time to Cook: 0 minutes

Yield: Servings 2

Ingredients:

- 1 tablespoon of ground flaxseeds
- 1 teaspoon of turmeric
- 2 cups of unsweetened almond milk
- 2 frozen bananas
- 2 tablespoons of raw cocoa powder
- 3 tablespoons of raw honey

Directions:

1. Combine all ingredients into a high-speed blender, and blend until the desired smoothness is achieved.
2. Split between two serving glasses, and enjoy straight away.

Nutritional Info: ‖ Total Carbohydrates: 74g ‖ Fiber: 7g ‖ Protein: 4g ‖ Total Fat: 6g ‖ Calories: 334

Vanilla Cakes

Time To Prepare*:* ten minutes

Time to Cook: fifteen minutes

Yield: Servings 8

Ingredients:

- .5 tsp. Baking soda
- .5 tsp. Salt
- 1 cup Agave sweetener
- 1 cup Almond milk
- 1 tbsp. Apple cider vinegar
- 2 cup Whole wheat flour
- 2 tsp. Baking powder
- C.5 cup warmed coconut oil
- tsp. Vanilla extract

Directions:

1. Ensure the oven is set to 350F.
2. Prepare two muffin pans (12 c) for use by greasing them.
3. Put in the apple cider vinegar into a measuring c that is big enough to hold minimum 2 c. Put in in the

almond milk for a total of 1.5 c. Allow the results to curdle roughly five minutes or until done.

4. Put together the salt, baking soda, baking powder, sugar, and flour together in a big container and whisk well.

5. Separately, mix the vanilla, coconut oil, and curdled almond in its container before combining the two bowls and blending well. Put in the results to the muffin pans, dividing uniformly.

6. Put the muffin pans in your oven and allow them to cook for approximately fifteen minutes. You will know if it's all already cook when you can press down on the tops and spring back when pressed lightly.

7. Allow the cake pans to cool on a wire rack before removing the cakes for the best results.

Nutritional Info: ‖ Calories: 336 kcal ‖ Protein: 5.75 g ‖ Fat: 16.25 g ‖ Carbohydrates: 44.15 g

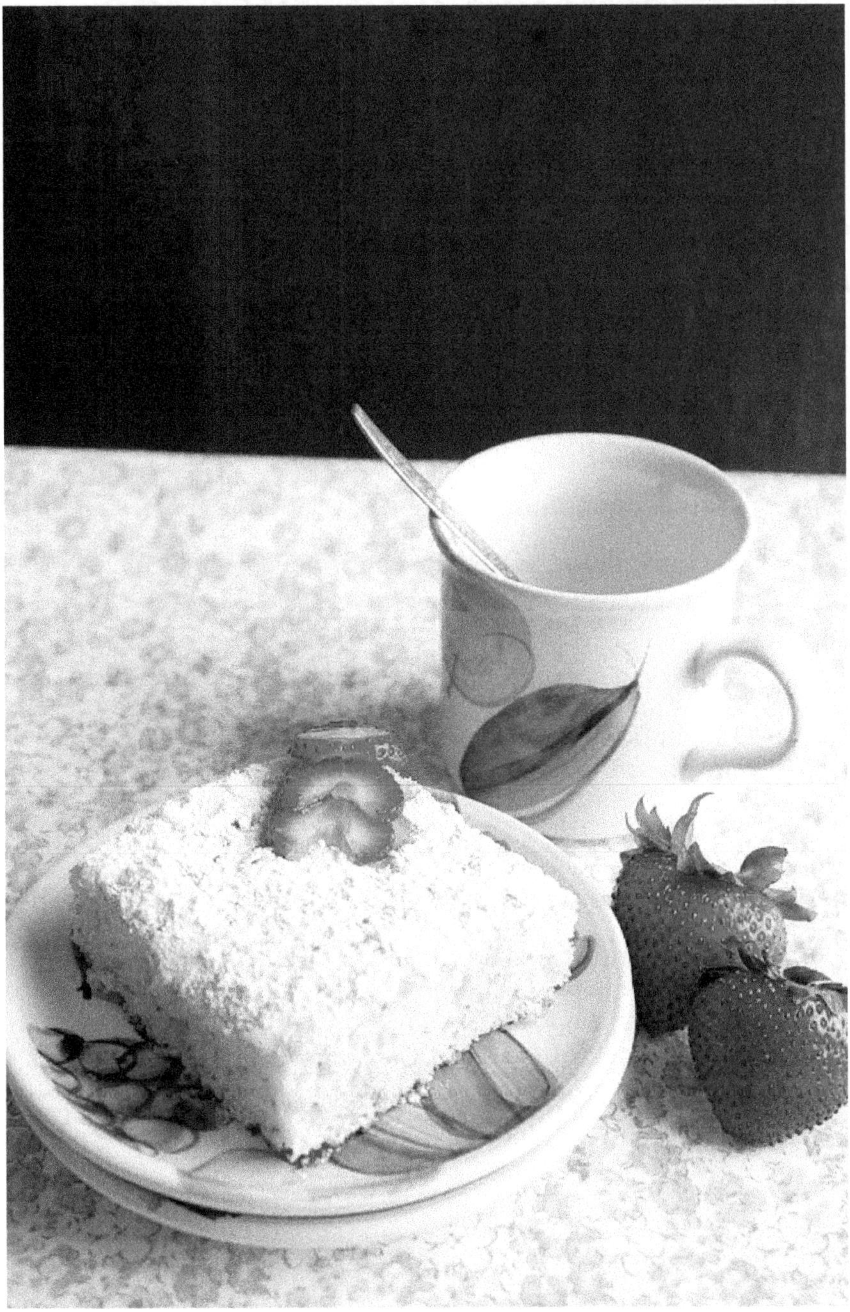

Watermelon and Avocado Cream

Time To Prepare: 2 hours
Time to Cook: 0 minutes
Yield: Servings 4

Ingredients:

- 1 tablespoon honey
- 1 watermelon, peeled and chopped
- 2 avocados, peeled, pitted and chopped
- 2 cups coconut cream
- 2 teaspoons lemon juice

Directions:

Throw all the ingredients into a blender. Split it into bowls, and keep in your refrigerator for about two hours before you serve.

Nutritional Info: Calories 121 ‖ Fat: 2 ‖ Fiber: 2 ‖ Carbohydrates: 6 ‖ Protein: 5

Watermelon Sorbet

Time To Prepare: 5 Minutes

Time to Cook: fifteen Minutes

Yield: Servings 4

Ingredients:

- 1 Seedless Watermelon, cubed

Directions:

1. To start with, put the watermelon cubes in a baking sheet in a uniform layer.
2. Next, keep the sheet in the freezer for about two hours or until the watermelon is solid.
3. After this, move the frozen watermelon cubes in the high-speed blender and puree them until you get a smooth puree.
4. Next, pour the puree among the two loaf pans.

Nutritional Info: ‖ Calories: 427Kcal ‖ Protein:5.9g ‖ Carbohydrates: 80g ‖ Fat: 15.6g

Yummy Fruity Ice-Cream

Time To Prepare: twenty minutes + 3-4 hours freezing

Time to Cook: 0 minutes

Yield: Servings 4

Ingredients:

- ½ cup of coconut cream
- ½ peeled and cut small banana
- 1 cup fresh strawberries, hulled and cut
- 2 tbsp. of shredded coconut

Directions:

1. In a powerful blender, put all together the ingredients and pulse till smooth.
2. Put it into an ice cream maker, then process in accordance with the manufacturer's directions.
3. Now, move into an airtight container. Freeze to set for minimum 3-4 hours, stirring after every thirty minutes.

Nutritional Info: ‖ Calories: 103 ‖ Fat: 8.2g ‖ Carbohydrates: 8.2g ‖ Protein: 1.2g ‖ Fiber: 2g

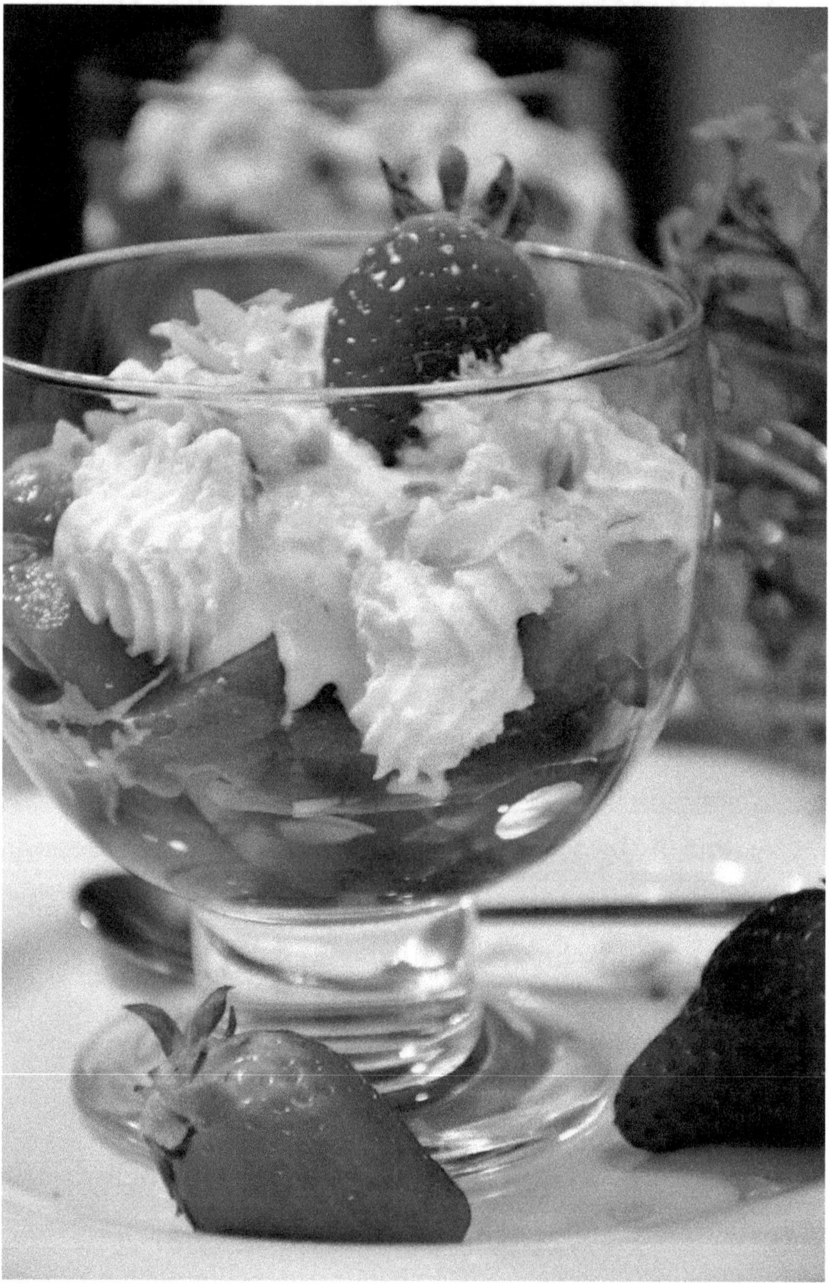

Lightning Source UK Ltd.
Milton Keynes UK
UKHW020114140123
415288UK00011B/142

9 781801 908382